The Hoof Balancer

Books by Jaime Jackson

The Natural Horse: Lessons from the Wild (1992, 2020)
Horse Owners Guide to Natural Hoof Care (1999)
Founder – Prevention and Cure the Natural Way (2001)
Guide To Booting Horses for Hoof Care Professionals (2002)
Paddock Paradise: A Guide to Natural Horse Boarding (2005)
The Natural Trim: Principles and Practice (2012)
Laminitis: An Equine Plague of Unconscionable Proportions (2016)
Training Manual: ISNHCP Natural Trim Training Program (2017)
The Natural Trim: Basic Guidelines (2019)
The Natural Trim: Advanced Guidelines (2019)

the Hoof Balancer

A Unique Tool for Balancing Equine Hooves

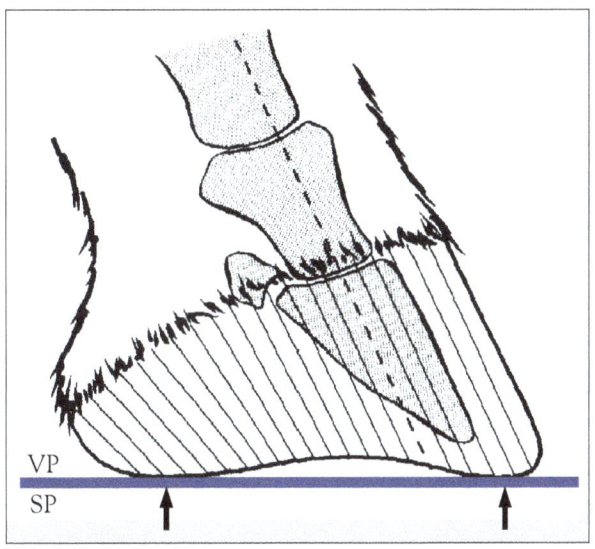

Instruction Guidelines
Using Natural Trim
Principles and Practices

Jaime Jackson

J. Jackson Publishing

©2017, 2020 Jaime Jackson
All rights reserved.

This book may not be reproduced in whole or in part, by any means (with the exception of short quotes for the purpose of review), without permission of the publisher.

Contact the author at:
J. Jackson Publishing
P.O. Box 1765
Harrison, AR 72602-1765
jjacksonpublishing@gmail.com

ISBN-13: 978-0-9848399-6-4

Natural hoof care is a sophisticated and highly technical process that should only be practiced by experienced natural hoof care professionals, or by persons under their immediate supervision. Neither the ISNHCP, the author, nor J. Jackson Publishing, accept responsibility for the applications or misapplications of these guidelines for using the *Hoof Balancer Tool*.

Contents

Introduction — About "Hoof Balance" 1

    About the Hoof Balancer Tool 1

    Hoof Balancer Tool and the ISNHCP Training Program for Natural Hoof Care Practitioners 2

Foundational Natural Hoof Care (NHC) Science based on the Wild Horse Model

    1 Active and Passive Wear Patterns of the Hoof Wall 3

    2 Navigational Landmarks and the Hoof Plexus 7

    3 Natural Heel Balance defined 11

    4 Natural Hoof Balance defined 16

Hoof Balancer Tool Instructions

    5 Natural Heel Balance: "Quick Method" 18

    6 Natural Hoof Balance (VP): "Quick Method" 19

    7 Natural Trim Recommendations 20

    8 Sighting Issues Due to Parallax 22

    9 Care of the Hoof Balancer Tool 23

Appendix

    Natural Horse Care Books by Jaime Jackson 24

    Jaime Jackson Online Store

        J. Jackson Professional Tripod Hoof Stand 26

        Professional Natural Trim Tools & Equipment 28

        J. Jackson Hay Poles and Hay Bags for Paddock Paradise 30

    NHC Social Media 32

    Image Credits 33

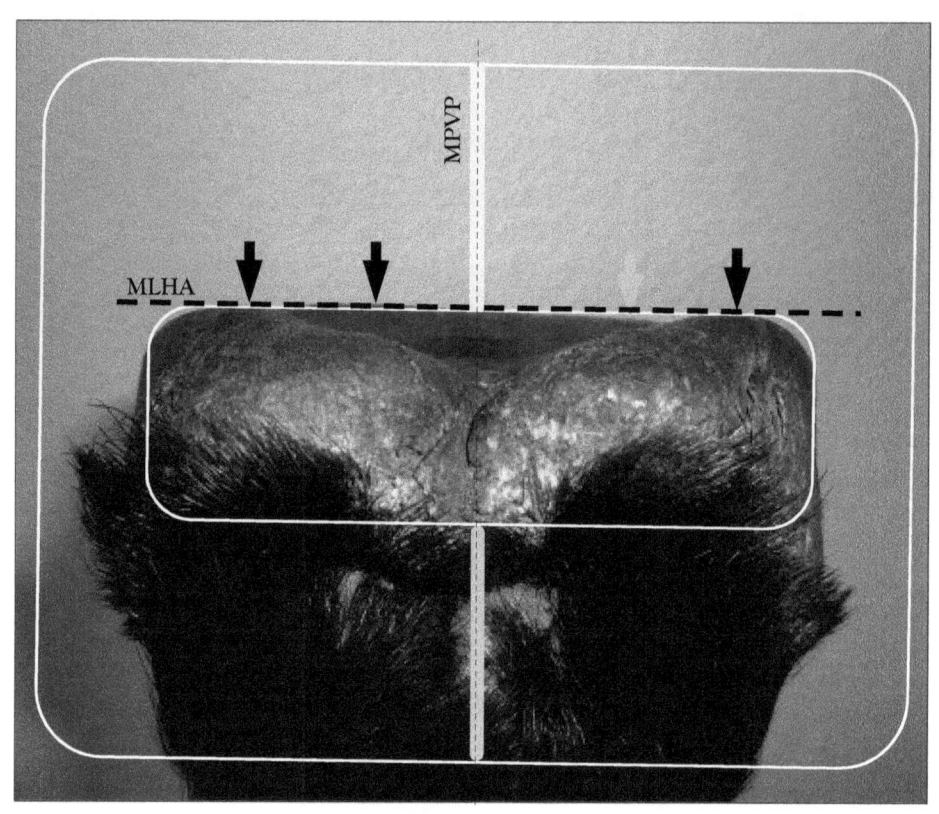

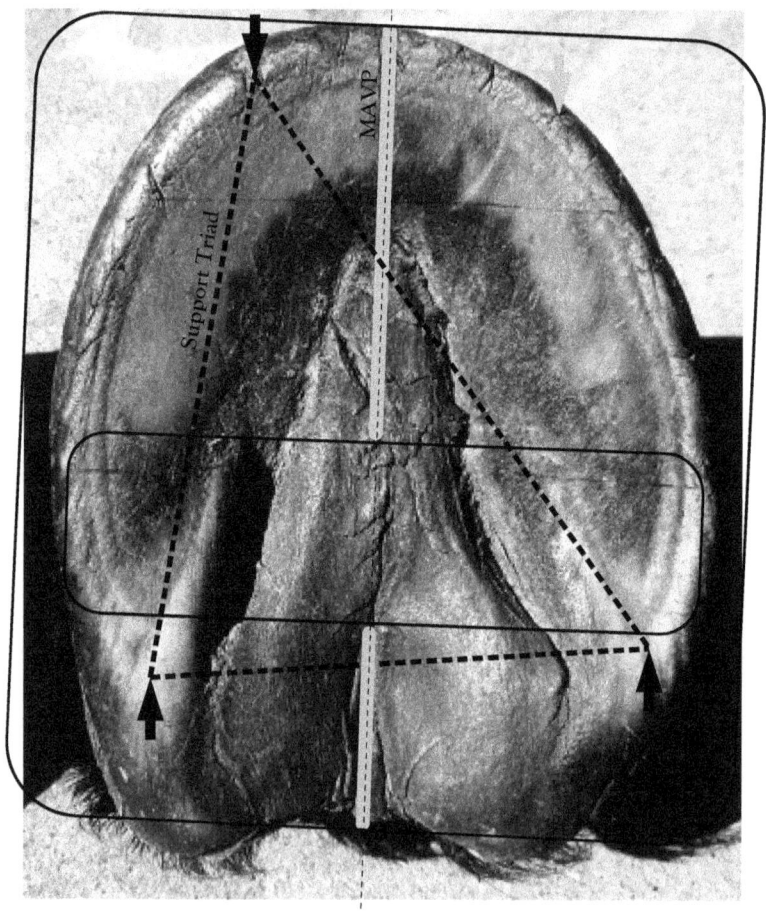

Introduction
About "Hoof Balance"

The meaning of "balanced hooves" in the hoof care world is rife with unsubstantiated opinions and methods that compromise the natural integrity of the hoof and the ability of the horse to move naturally. Few agree on toe length, heel length, relative heel position to the frog, relative positions of the heel buttresses within the hoof's volar profile, relative lengths of the medial and lateral heels, front heels versus hind heels, active or passive heel length, heel length in relation to the heel bulbs, on and on. Moreover, this widespread technical disparity continues endlessly by breed, competition, gait, and even hoof color!

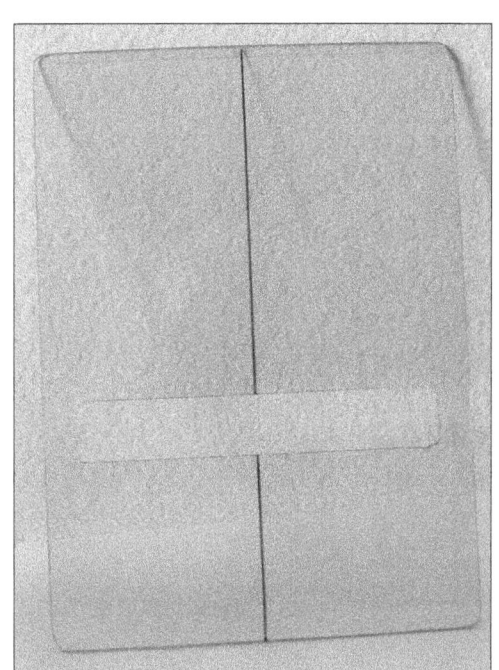

Hoof Balancer tool.

The wild horse model is clear, however, that there shouldn't be this type of incongruity at all. Nature has demonstrated unequivocally what the relationships are between the toe, quarters, heels and other structures of the hoof. Balancing the hoof, therefore, should never be left to chance, even with the most deformed hooves. Indeed, the complexities of capsule wryness, slipper toe, bull-nose, club foot, and under trimmed heels require that we have a clear path to balancing the hoof whatever its unnatural orientation.

About the Hoof Balancer Tool

The *Hoof Balancer tool* provides us with a quick, easy, accurate, and efficient way to balance the hoof when conducting the natural trim. It is a great learning tool for students when deployed on both cadaver and live hooves, but is also recommended for use by all hoof care practitioners in the field, particularly when confronted with extreme capsule deformity.

The Hoof Balancer is used for two purposes: to determine the location of *active* and *passive wear* in the hoof's Volar Plane, which define *natural hoof balance*; and in sighting and marking the *Mediolateral Heel Axis* (MLHA), which defines *heel balance*. In either case, a working understanding of *active and passive wear* (Chapter 1) and the *Navigational Landmarks* (Chapter 2) are recommended to use the *Hoof Balancer* according to its fullest potential in the course of conducting the natural trim.

The Hoof Balancer can be used at any time during the course of the natural trim. In fact, it is highly recommended that it be deployed before

A "Brumby" – The wild, free-roaming horse of the Australian Outback with naturally shaped hooves.

any trimming commences with any hoof. And in such cases, it is wise to use it preceding each "nipper run" if lowering the hoof wall in increments is indicated by copious and/or deformed growth. Students should use it before any nipper run. And, for all hoof care practitioners, it can be used as a tool to check their work on any hoof when balance is in question and confirmation is necessary.

The Hoof Balancer Tool and the ISNHCP Natural Trim Training Program for Natural Hoof Care Practitioners

The Hoof Balancer tool was created specifically for the ISNHCP Training Program for NHC practitioners. This book was written for instructional purposes as part of the training program. Learn more about this important training program, and other related learning materials in this book's appendix.

Chapter One
Active and Passive Wear Patterns of the Hoof Wall

Active and *passive wear patterns* are the unique contours of the hoof wall's ground-bearing surface. Unlike the "flat" hoof wall that is shod, the naturally shaped hoof wall is not only not flat, but is very distinct in terms of which parts are actively supporting the entire hoof and which parts are not! Meaning, certain segments of the wall are more protruding than others. But what exactly is meant by "active" and "passive?"

The more protruding segments are defined as "active wear" or "support pillars"; areas of recession between active wear are defined as "passive wear" (*Figure 1-1*). There's an analogy with people who go barefoot: areas of active wear (like the ball or heel of the human foot) typically are callused; areas of passive wear (e.g., the arch of the foot) tend to be less callused or not callused at all. Active wear for both our species are an epidermal response to greater wear forces. This is nature's way of protecting — and, as it turns out — balancing our feet.

Active wear is associated with *active support*, whereas passive wear means

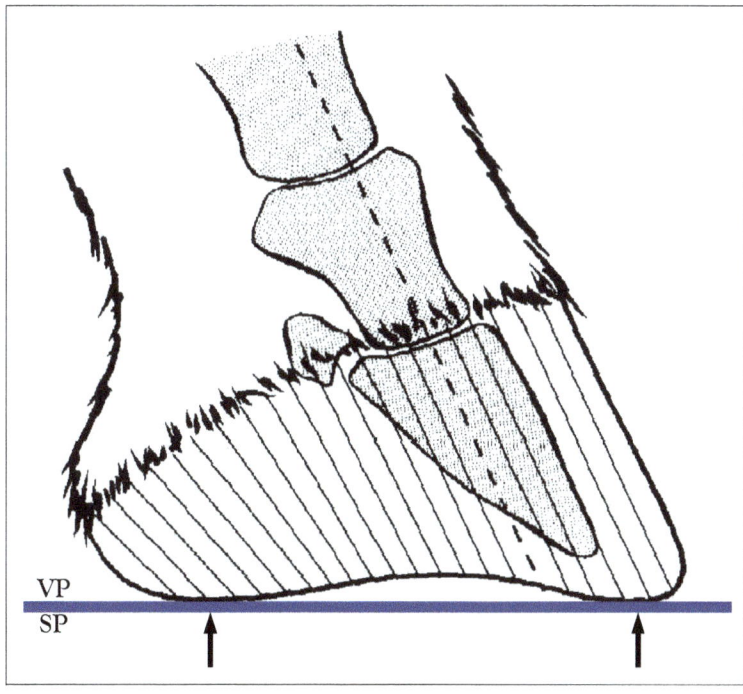

Figure 1-1. *Arrows* point to segments of active wear ("support pillars"). The expanse of hoof wall between the support pillars is defined as passive wear ("passive support").

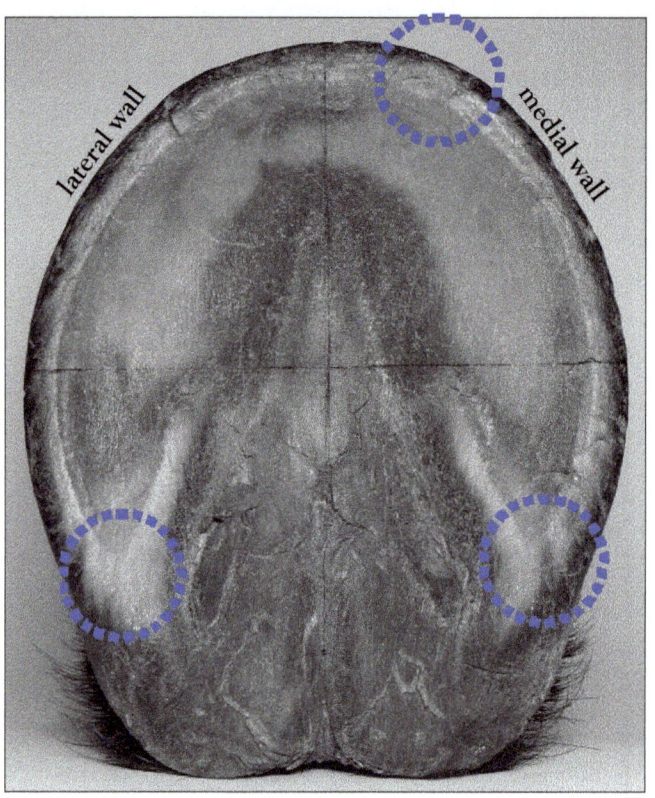

Figure 1-2. Dashed circles mark the location of *active wear* ("active support") over both heels and one segment on the medial toe wall.

Figure 1-3. Arrow points to *active wear pillar* on medial toe wall.

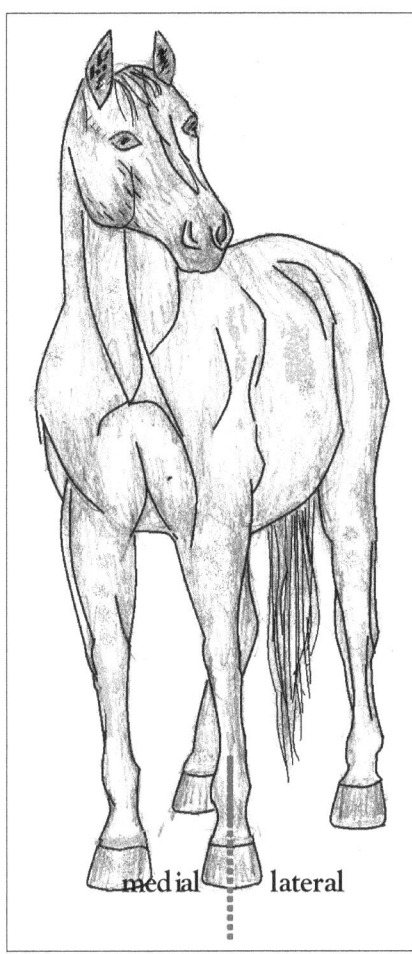

Figure 1-4. The medial wall of the hoof is the side closest to the horse's spine. The lateral wall lies away from the spine.

*This is a rather elaborate term I have coined to describe the natural gaits and those elements of basic locomotive biomechanics that make the gaits what they are, specifically: collection, footfall sequences, leads, stride and stride extension, rhythm, tempo, cadence, and suspension. Simplified: how horses naturally move without human influence.

passive support. Specific areas of active (and passive) wear are technically defined by the relationship of the hoof's *volar plane* to a hypothetical *support plane*. The support plane (SP) is any flat surface that can support the horse's hoof, such as a flat board. The angle of a SP is not important, only that it is flat. The volar plane (VP) is the plane formed by the hoof's active wear pillars when the hoof is standing on a SP. Thus, active wear along the VP makes physical contact with the SP, passive wear does not. The blue line in Figure 1-1 represents the SP; the hoof's support pillars form the VP. Significantly, what this means is that SP technically defines VP.

The naturally balanced hoof – derived from the wild horse model of the U.S. Great Basin – has three areas of active wear, that is, three support pillars: both heels and one segment of the toe wall (*Figure 1-2*). Moreover, with few exceptions, toe wall pillars occur on the medial side of the hoof (*Figure 1-3*). The medial side of the hoof is the side closest to the horse's spine (*Figure 1-4*). Because they typically occur in groups of three (medial toe wall and both heels), they are also called *support triads* (*Figure 1-5*).

Active and passive wear are significant characteristics of the naturally shaped hoof. In fact, active wear technically defines *hoof balance*, providing the hoof has been otherwise trimmed to ISNHCP guidelines for the natural trim based on the wild horse model. One might ask: Why is there active and passive wear? Why isn't the hoof just flat like a horseshoe (since that is the way horses are shod)? And why does the toe wall pillar typically occur along the medial toe wall?

My opinion is that this is due to variation of the species in terms of their great diversity of temperaments, conformations, and other traits. All of these influences, along with their ancient adaptive environment (exemplified by the Great Basin), collectively flow through the species *natural gait complex*.* Active and passive wear, as a consequence, are extruded through the natural gaits. Active wear pillars, for example, reflect areas of increased locomotive (weight-bearing) forces on the hoof wall; conversely, passive wear less so. Within the horse's foot, the dermis (*coronary corium*) that creates the hoof wall, responding through its nerve bed, produces more epidermis (forming the pillars of the support triad) to offset wear and sustain the horse's balance – less the hoof grow awry and imperil the natural gaits altogether. Areas of passive wear, logically, are fortified with less epidermal armor because there is less locomotive force in those expanses of the hoof wall. The presence of the horseshoe "short circuits" the dermal-

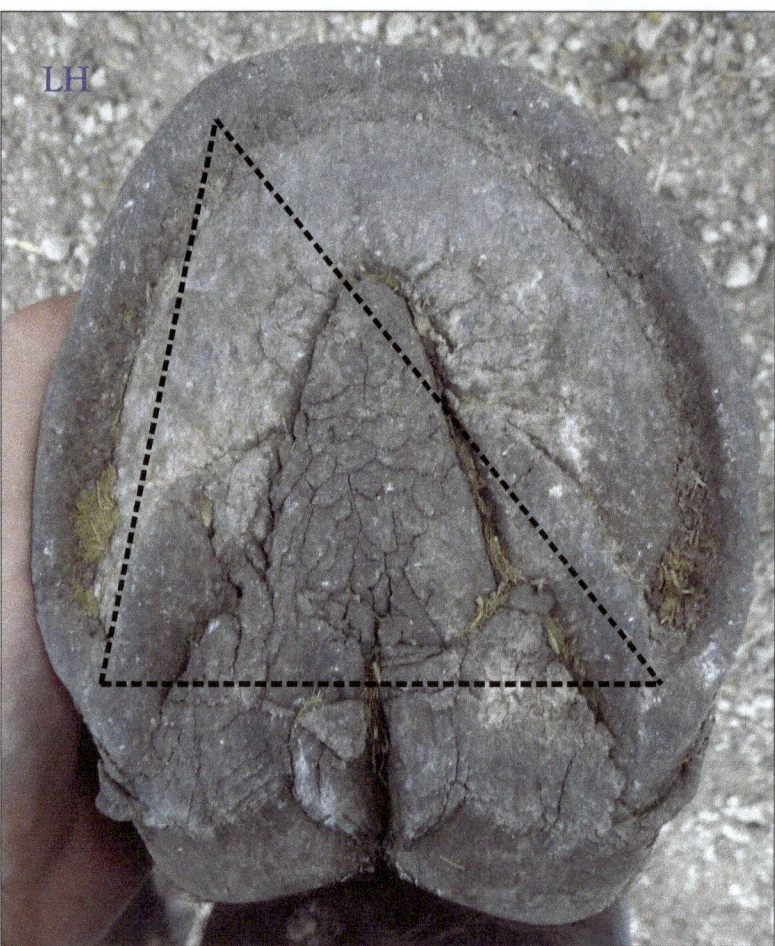

Figure 1-5. Points of the triangle mark the location of this left hind hoof's *support pillars*; collectively, these pillars form a *support triad*.

epidermal nerve-based "information" exchange, precluding the foot's ability to generate active and passive wear. This inability of the foot to adjust its growth patterns to facilitate natural hoof balance, and, consequently, locomotive balance, unquestionably can be traced to ligament, tendon, and muscle damage across the horse's body. Navicular Syndrome is clearly one catastrophic example.[1]

---

[1] *Navicular Syndrome* (NS): (Pathology) NHC definition — any severe trauma injury to the horse's body above the hoof, resulting in a clubfoot in one of the front feet, and a limp over the clubfoot when moving in a turn at the trot. NS commonly arises from horses ridden repetitively outside the biomechanical limits of the natural gait complex. Jaime Jackson. *The Natural Trim: Principles and Practice* (2012, rev. 2019) p. 238.

Chapter Two
Navigational Landmarks and the Hoof Plexus

The *Navigational Landmarks* are very targeted lines drawn on the hoof. Specifically, they form a grid, that is, a network of horizontal and perpendicular lines, planes, and points that facilitate the measuring of "lengths" and "angles" – data that would be useful in trimming the hoof according to the wild horse model. This grid-works is called the *Hoof Plexus** (*Figure 2-1*). The hoof plexus is of foundational importance in conducting the natural trim, and, specifically, in balancing the hoof using the Hoof Balancer tool. Of the many landmarks gridding the hoof plexus, only three are necessary to gauge hoof balance with the tool: the *MAVP*, *MPVP* and *MLHA*.

*Plexus: an interwoven combination of parts or elements in a structure or system.

Medial Axis of the Volar Profile (MAVP)

The *Medial Axis of the Volar Profile*, or MAVP, is a line that we draw down

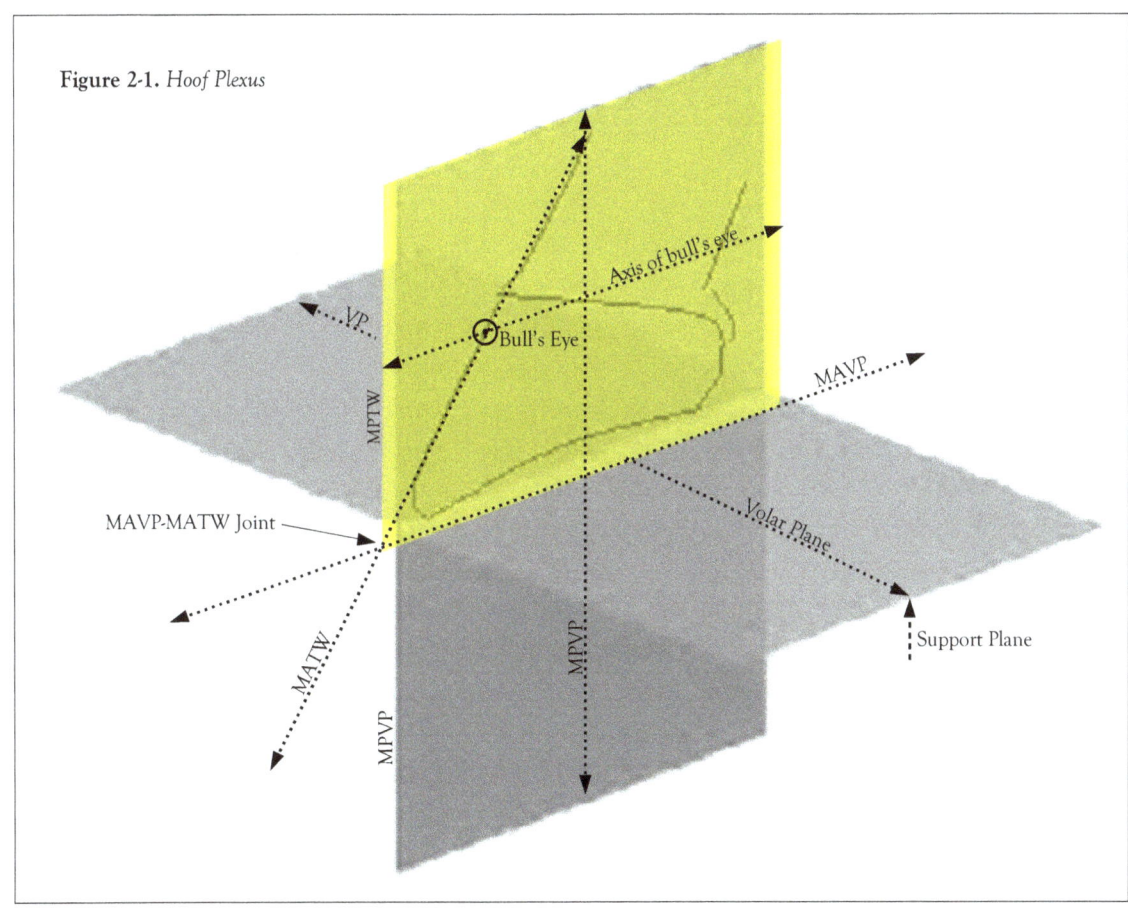

Figure 2-1. *Hoof Plexus*

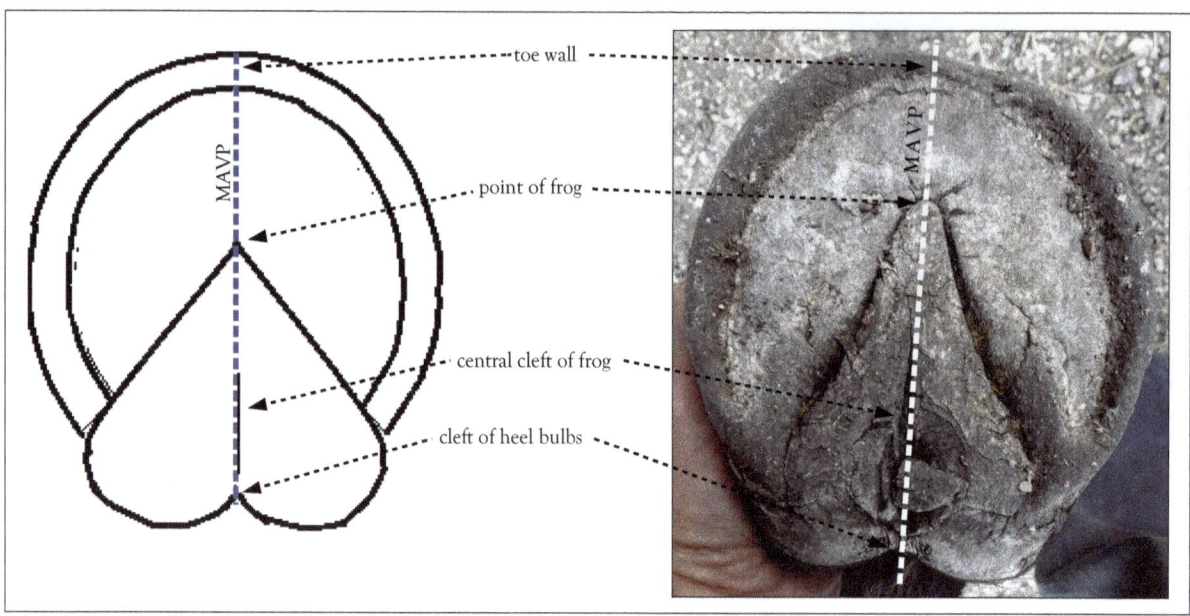

Figure 2-2. *Marking the MAVP:* Draw a line with a Sharpie pen down the middle of the bottom of the hoof. The line should pass through the cleft of the heel bulbs, the central cleft of the frog, and the point of frog. Extend the line all the way to the toe wall. This line is called the *Medial Axis of the Volar Profile* (MAVP). "Medial Axis" means "a line down the middle." "Volar Profile" means "a representation of the bottom of the hoof."

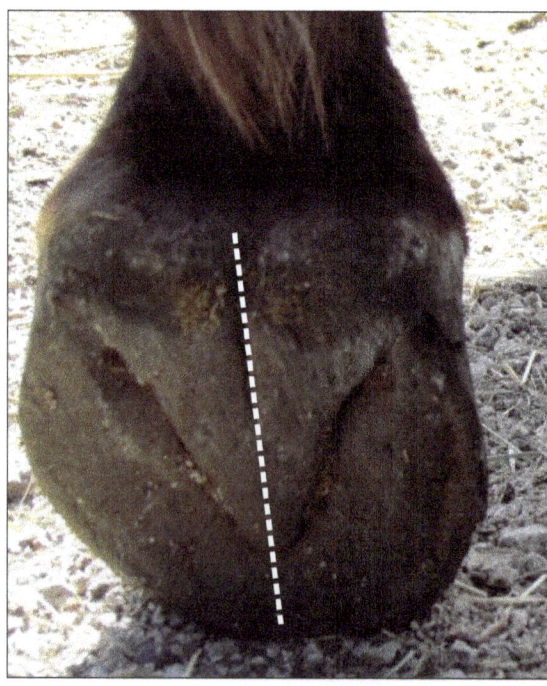

Figure 2-3. *Marking the MAVP: other* examples of where the MAVP would be drawn on the bottom of the hoof. These are the naturally shaped hooves of horses living in Paddock Paradise at the AANHCP Field Headquarters in the coastal mountains of central California.*

*Association for the Advancement of Natural Hoof Care Practitioners (www.AANHCP.net).

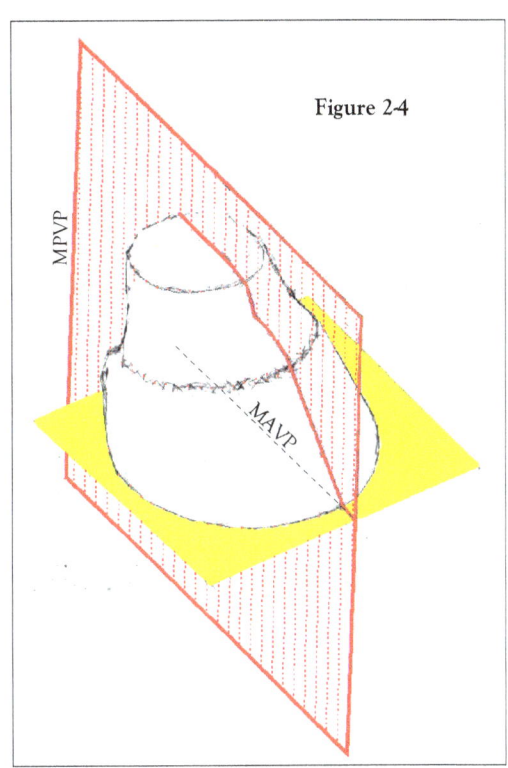

Figure 2-4

the center of the bottom of the hoof, dividing it lengthwise into two — medial and lateral — halves (*Figure 2-2* and *Figure 2-3*). The MAVP is a one-dimensional line which passes through three strategically important landmarks: *cleft of the heel bulbs*, *central cleft (sulcus) of the frog*, and the *point-of-frog* (also called the *frog apex*). In Chapters 4 and 6, we will lay the *Hoof Balancer* on the bottom of the hoof and align it with the MAVP. This will enable us to locate the hoof wall's support pillars and evaluate the VP for hoof balance.

Median Plane of the Volar Profile (MPVP)

The *Median Plane of the Volar Profile*, or MPVP, is an imaginary two-dimensional plane of the *Hoof Plexus* that passes through and is aligned with the MAVP (*Figure 2-1* and *Figure 2-4*). Significantly, by definition of the Hoof Plexus, the MPVP lies at right angles* to both the SP and the VP (review *Figure 1-3*).

Technically, the MPVP necessarily supersedes the MAVP when evaluating *heel balance*. This is because the Hoof Balancer tool isn't laid directly upon the bottom of the hoof so as to align with the MAVP in order to evaluate the VP. Instead, it is held at the back of the hoof at an angle and then aligned with the same reference points that also define the MAVP: *cleft of the heel bulbs*, *central cleft (sulcus) of the frog*, and the *point of frog*. Having said this, to the extent that the MAVP drawn across the bottom of the hoof is visible, it is also used to align the Hoof Balancer tool to locate the MPVP.** Although conceptually abstract, using the tool will bring clarity.

Mediolateral Heel Axis (MLHA)

The *Mediolateral Heel Axis* (MLHA) is a horizontal cut-line drawn across the back of both heels and the frog. The MLHA lies at a right angle (90°) to the MPVP (*Figure 2-5* and *Figure 2-6*). It is also perpendicular (90°) to the SP (in keeping with the Hoof Plexus); therefore, it is also parallel with the ground. Thus, the MLHA defines *heel balance* and, in conjunction with the medial toe wall pillar, is also a key player in establishing overall natural *hoof balance*. This too may seem abstract but using the tool will help you to see these relationships.

It is both fascinating and ironic that the structural complexities of the naturally balanced wild horse hoof, which borders on chaos to the untrained eye, is, in fact, a masterpiece of multidimensional orderliness. Equally important, when interpreted through the lens of the Hoof Plexus, nature provides a direct pathway to order in the very worst deformed hoof.

*"Right angle to" is synonymous with: perpendicular to, ninety degrees to, 90° to, and ↱.

**Speaking the acronymic language of the Navigational Landmarks (and the Critical Measurements) can be a bit mind-boggling at first. But once confirmed through practice with the Balancer Tool at the hoof, it is easy to follow and precludes the tediousness of enunciating everything word by word!

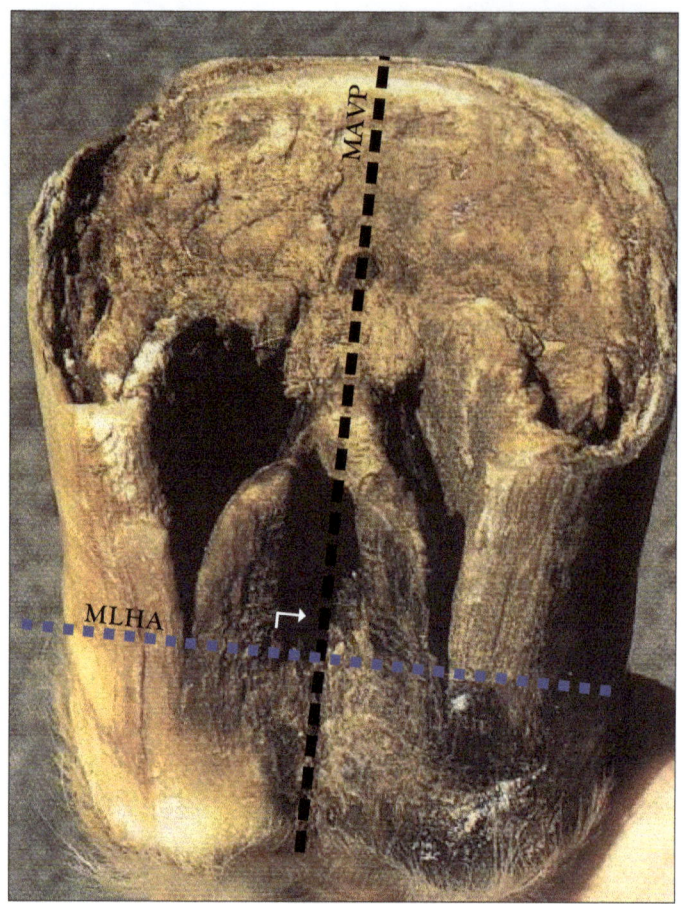

Figure 2-5. The MLHA relative to the MPVP in a severely neglected hoof.

Figure 2-6. The MLHA relative to the VP, MPVP and the *support triad* in a naturally shaped hoof trimmed to natural trim guidelines for 8 consecutive years.

Chapter Three
Natural Heel Balance

Locating the *Mediolateral Heel Axis* (MLHA) is a critical step of the natural trim in determining or finding one's way to *natural heel balance*. The MLHA and medial toe wall pillar serve together to balance the hoof anteroposteriorly (front to back). With the MPVP, the MLHA balances the hoof mediolaterally (side to side) by determining heel lengths relative to the VP. The question arises, why is this so? The answer is that these relationships given to natural hoof balance are axiomatic (self-evident) as they are derived from the wild horse model itself. Examples:

1. The MPVP is "fixed" by the horse's DNA and does not change throughout the horse's life, whether wild, domesticated, naturally balanced or manifestly corrupted by human mismanagement.
2. The MPVP and the SP are intersecting planes (at 90°) in three-dimensional space.
3. The MLHA lies at right angles to the MPVP *and* is parallel to the SP.
4. By default, the VP is rendered parallel to the SP by the MLHA.

The wild horse model dictates further that the natural trim guidelines are *not* concerned with:

5. The relative locations of the heels either toward or away from the MAVP.
6. The relative locations of the heels either toward or away from the medial toe wall pillar.
7. The actual measurable lengths of the heels from the coronary band to the SP.

Nature is unequivocally revealing of much variation in these relationships. Instead, the natural trim guidelines are concerned only with heel length — whatever each might be — relative to the MLHA. This is true of the most naturally shaped hoof and the most deformed.

Without the *Hoof Plexus*, there would be no logical way to deduce natural heel balance. The vagaries of domestication completely obscure the native positions of the heels seen in the wild. Indeed, both *hoof balance* and *heel balance* are rendered into self-serving mumbo-jumbo equally among farriers, vets, generic barefooters, and horse owners. The Hoof Balancer tool elucidates the mystery as quick as the user is able to bring it to the hoof and apply the Sharpie. With sufficient experience, the user may be able to develop an "eye" to see natural heel balance or the absence of without the Hoof Balancer tool in all but the most deformed hooves.

Applying the Hoof Balancer Tool

In the following instructions, I have applied a simulated Balancer tool to: 1) a wild horse hoof, 2) a hoof that has been shaped at the AANHCP Paddock Paradise that closely approximates the Great Basin, and 3) a cadaver specimen from a domesticated horse revealing neglect.

Wild horse hoof

This left hind, Great Basin wild horse hoof (*Figure 3-1*, a freeze-dried cadaver specimen) is revealing of natural heel balance I documented among Great Basin wild horses. The wild hoof generally presents certain challenges to decipher heel balance from it. But it is worth the effort in establishing a firm foundation for determining heel balance in the hooves of domesticated horses, particularly those suffering from severe hoof deformities.

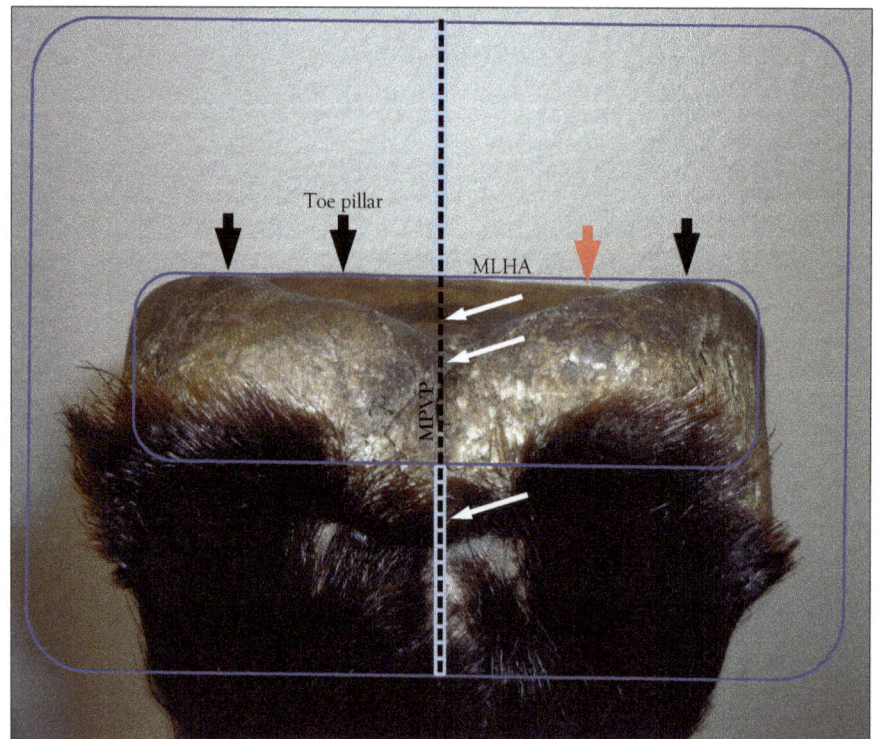

Figure 3-1. *Left hind wild horse hoof.* The groove of the simulated Balancer tool has been aligned with the MPVP. The MLHA follows along the upper edge of the Balancer tool's window. *Black solid arrows* point to triad of support pillars. *Red arrow* points to passive toe wall. *White arrows* approximate in descending positions the *point of frog, central frog sulcus*, and *cleft of heel bulbs*. Figure 3-2 shows their relative positions in the hoof's volar profile. Technically, in this view, the MLHA and VP are aligned with each other, and theoretically, also with the SP.

Layer upon layer of highly callused frog epidermis render it nearly impossible to distinguish the frog from the heels, nor one frog bulb from the other, in this posterior view — typical of wild horse hooves. But this is no problem as only the 3 support pillars relative to the MPVP are necessary to find the MLHA and, from there, ascertain heel balance.

Natural Heel Balance

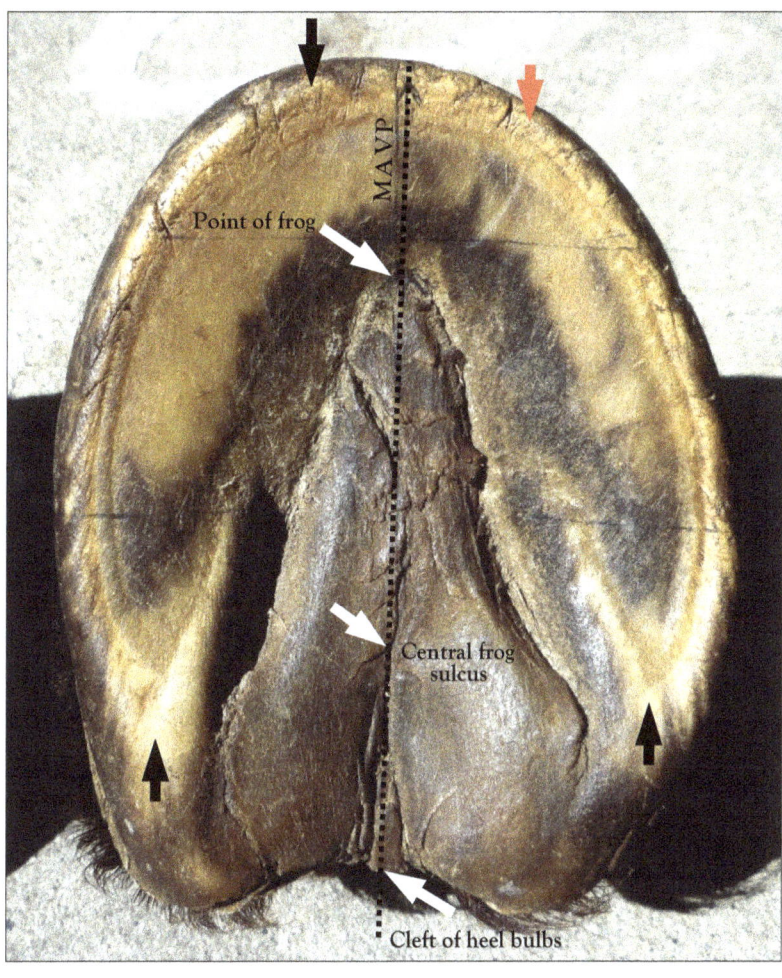

Figure 3-2. This is the same left hind wild hoof seen in Figure 3-1. *Black solid arrows* point to support pillars. *Red arrow* points to passive lateral toe wall. *White arrows* identify the *point of frog, central frog sulcus,* and *cleft of heel bulbs*.

AANHCP Paddock Paradise hoof

Natural wear, the natural trim, and life "on track" in a very challenging Paddock Paradise, converged to forge this left hind hoof into a very near wild state (*Figure 3-3*).

Figure 3-3. The MLHA follows along the lower window edge of a portion of the simulated Balancer tool. *Black solid arrows* point to tips of support pillars that form the VP. *Red arrow* points to passive lateral toe wall. *Black dashed arrows* approximate in descending positions the *point of frog, central frog sulcus,* and *cleft of heel bulbs*.

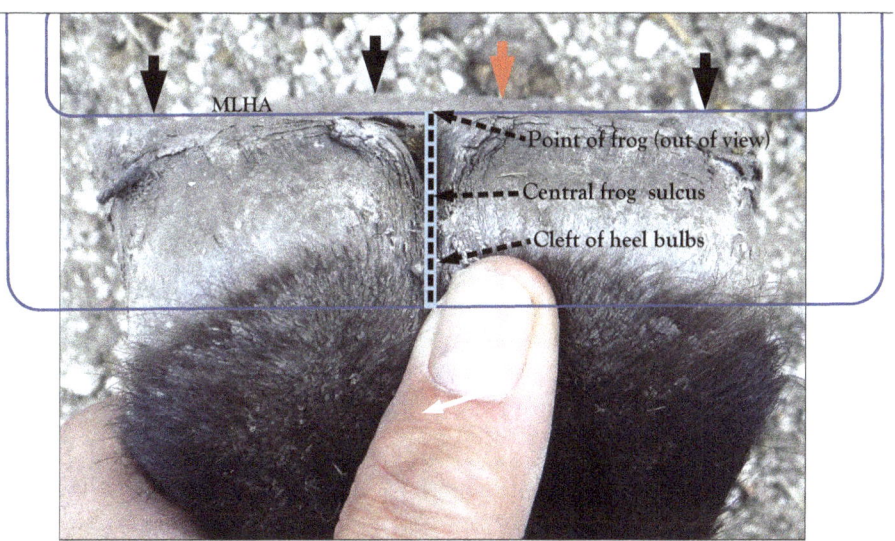

13

Neglected hoof and Frog Notching

This hoof has extremely long heels (*Figure 3-4*), but the Balancer tool still facilitates a close approximation of the MLHA prior to trimming. The final location of the MLHA (to achieve heel balance) is subject to change if the heels and frog will require further lowering. A natural trim technique called "frog notching" is used to make this determination (*Figures 3-5* and *3-6*).

Figure 3-4. Cadaver hoof. The MPVP and groove of the Balancer tool are aligned. The *lower edge* of the tool's window is laid against the neglected heels of the hoof seen earlier in *Figure 2-4*. *Dashed blue line* marks the location of the MLHA. In life, we draw the MLHA with a black-inked Sharpie pen, tracing along the lower edge of the window. This forms a cutline across both heels and the frog. The lengths of the *white double arrows* suggest frog notching will be necessary to confirm actual heel length and the possible need to lower the MLMA further with additional trimming (*Figure 3-5*).

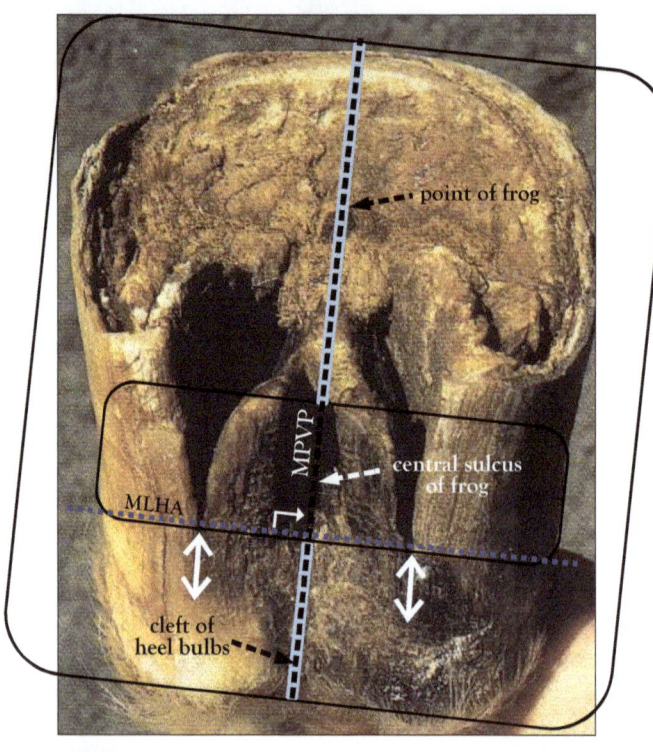

Figure 3-5. Cadaver hoof. *Black box* focuses on the "notch," wherein the posterior-most length of the frog near the heel buttress is trimmed down to the base of the heel wall with the nipper or hoof knife. The resulting notch, which forms a "V" between the heel wall and the frog (*dashed black lines*), exposes the true length of the heel wall. To experienced trimmers this is important information in helping to determine if the heel-buttresses (i.e., the medial and lateral support pillars) are lowered enough to set the MLHA (*blue dashed line*). Notching on live horses is only recommended for experienced trimmers trained with cadaver hooves.

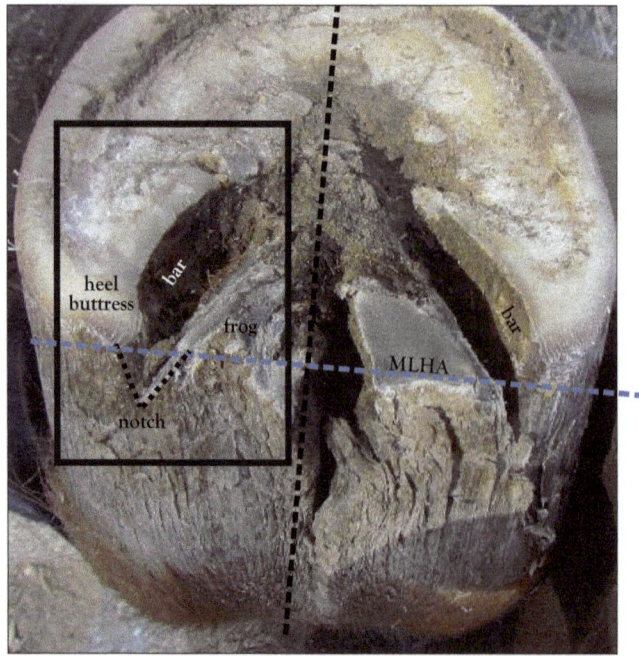

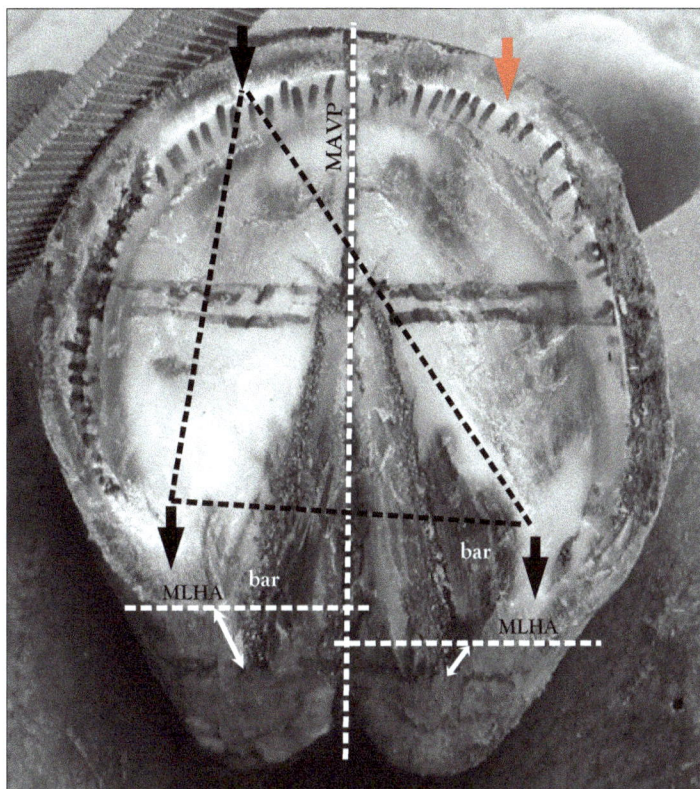

Figure 3-6. *Left front cadaver hoof.* This is an interesting — and not uncommon — example of the MLHA intersecting the MAVP (*medial axis of the volar profile*) in two different locations, yet forming a single axis when the hoof is viewed in its posterior profile and aligning with the MPVP (e.g., *Figure 3-1* and *Figure 3-3*). The explanation is actually simple and worth thinking through as it is likely to happen to anyone working with horse hooves. First, a few important observations:
- The triad formed by *black dashed lines* indicates this is a left front hoof.
- The MAVP passes through the *central sulcus of the frog.*
- The medial and lateral lengths of the frog have been trimmed back ("notched") exposing the bars and heel lengths at the back of the hoof.
- *White double arrows* trace the lengths of the medial and lateral heel walls.
- The *medial double arrow* is longer but at a lower angle (slope) than the *lateral double arrow*. Thus, the medial heel and its support pillar lie further forward than the lateral heel and support pillar. (Refer back to page 11, #5 through #7.)

What all of this means is that the Balancer tool will have to lay across the lateral heel wall when sighting and aligning with the MPVP. The Sharpie pen will have to extend further to reach the medial wall in this example. If just sighting the MLHA by an experienced eye alone, then it's a simpler matter.

Chapter Four
Natural Hoof Balance

Active wear in naturally shaped hooves, we have seen, always occurs at both heel buttresses and typically a single point on the medial toe wall (e.g., *Figures 1-2* and *1-5*] forming *support triads*. These triads form on both front and hind hooves. When the heels are naturally balanced, the triads help define *natural hoof balance*. Over trimmed heels that do not make contact with SP, or a hoof whose medial toe wall is passive to the lateral toe wall are not naturally balanced. However, if either or both is the case, they will correct over time with the natural trim. The trimmer should note this in their records for the horse.

Applying the Hoof Balancer tool

Place the Balancer tool on the bottom of the hoof and align its grooved line with the MAVP (*Figure 4-1*). The *Hoof Balancer* will now be resting upon the hoof's *volar plane* (VP).* *Active and passive wear* can now be located by passing a piece of paper or thin object between the hoof wall and the Balancer tool. Active wear (support pillars) will make contact with the paper, passive wear will not. The frog should be level with the tool (i.e., making contact) or just passive to it (making no contact).

*The tool can be said to be acting as the SP.

Summary

If the heels are naturally balanced as explained in Chapter 3, and the volar plane is formed from a support triad as explained above, then the hoof is said to be naturally balanced. When this is not the case, nature is very forgiving when the natural trim is applied, and in due time will assert new growth (called "mass migrations") where it is needed to establish balance.

Natural Hoof Balance

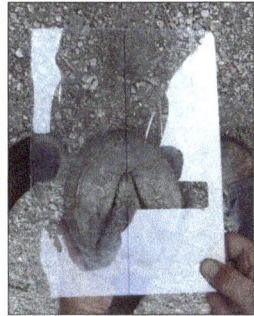

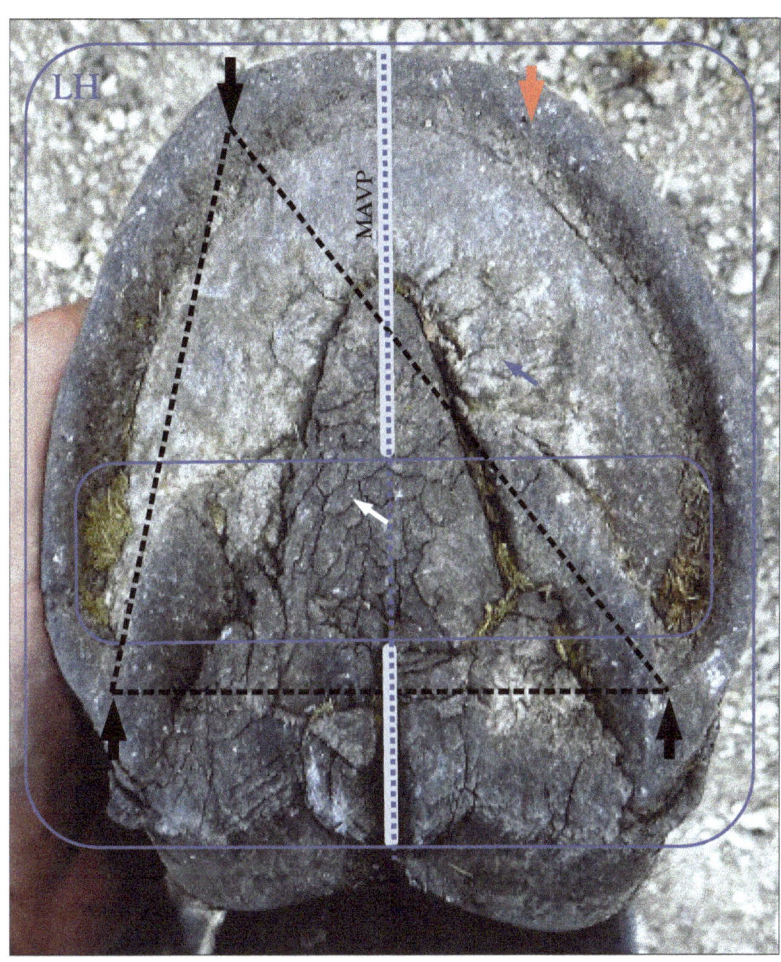

Figure 4-1.
(*Above*) Naturally shaped left hind hoof (AANHCP Paddock Paradise). I've applied the Balancer tool to check for hoof balance prior to trimming.
(*Right*) Same hoof as above. Grooved centerline of simulated Balancer tool is aligned with the MAVP (*dashed blue line*). *Black arrows* point to support pillars; *red arrow* points to passive lateral toe wall. *Dashed black lines* articulate to identify the *support triad*. A piece of paper will slide under the *Balancer tool* anywhere between the support pillars along the hoof wall. Compare with Figure 4-2.

Worth noting at right also are the numerous small flaps of frog epidermis (*white arrow*). These constitute the "hard frog plane," analogous to the "hard sole plane" (*blue arrow*). These flaps emerge and shed naturally and are not trimmed off, except in cases of neglect, as they are an important protective barrier.

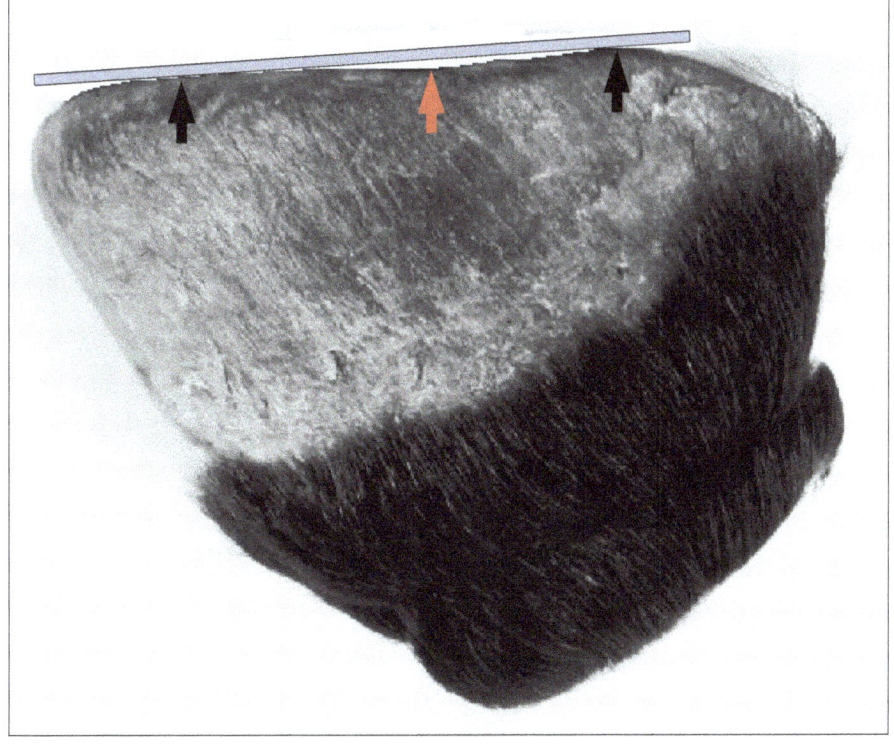

Figure 4-2. Simulated Balancer laid on the VP of a wild horse hoof showing active (*black arrows*) and passive (*red arrow*) wear.

Chapter Five
Natural Heel Balance: "Quick Method"

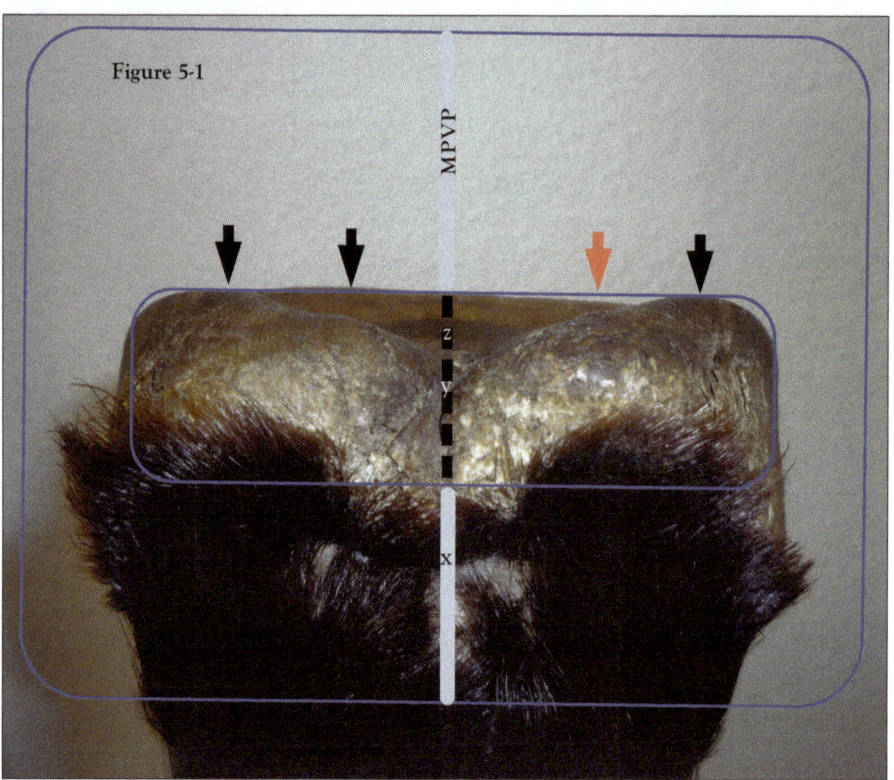

*When learning to find the MPVP, you may find it helpful to first draw the MAVP on the bottom of the hoof with a Sharpie.

Figure 5-1. *Left hind wild horse hoof.* This is a quick way to determine *natural heel balance*. By "quick," I mean this takes less than a minute.

1. Hold *Hoof Balancer* against the heel bulbs. If one bulb is protruding more than the other, lay it against the one more protruding as explained in Figure 3-6.

2. Line up the grooved line of the Balancer tool with the *central cleft of the heel bulbs* [x], the *central cleft of frog* [y], and the *point of frog* [z]. The Balancer tool is now aligned with the MPVP.*

3. Raise or lower the upper edge of the Balancer tool's window until it lines up with both heel wall pillars and the forward toe wall pillar in a single plane. *Red arrow* points to passive wear area of lateral toe wall; you should expect to see this even if it is very subtle.

4. In Chapter 8, I explain some precautions you'll need to take when maneuvering the Balancer tool to sight the hoof. These concern what are called *parallax shifts* that can distort one's view of the hoof. So you might want to skip to that chapter right now and study the examples to avoid these problems from arising.

18

Chapter Six
Natural Hoof Balance: "Quick Method"

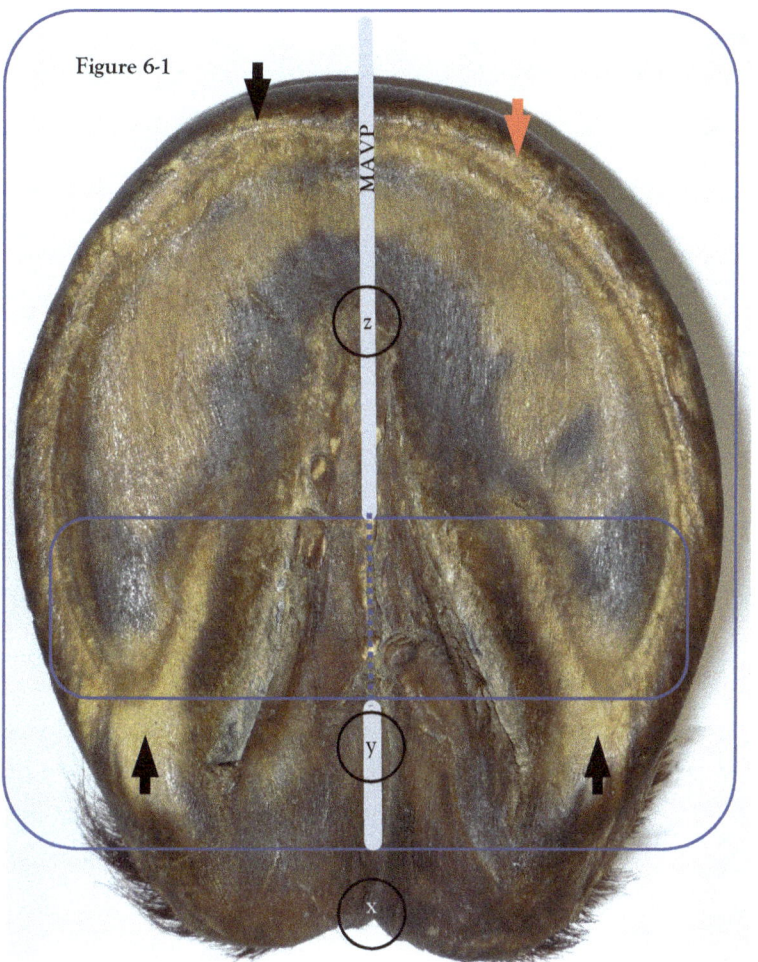

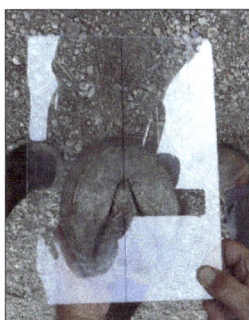

Figure 6-1. *Left front wild horse hoof.* This is a quick way to determine *natural hoof balance.*

1. Place the Balancer tool on the bottom of the hoof. Line up the grooved line of the Balancer tool with the *cleft of the heel bulbs* [x], the *central sulcus of the frog* [y], and the *point of frog* [z]. The Balancer tool is now aligned with the MAVP.

2. Pass a corner of a piece of paper or other paper-thin object between the hoof wall and the Balancer tool. Locate the support pillars which will block the paper.

3. A naturally balanced hoof will have three support pillars: both heels and one pillar on the medial toe wall (i.e., the side closest to the horse's spine, as seen in Figure 1-4). *Red arrow* points to passive wear area of lateral toe wall; you should expect to see this even if it is very subtle.

4. Parallax shifts are not an issue here.

Chapter 7
Natural Trim Recommendations

Below and on the facing page is a brief explanation of the principal hoof structures to be trimmed to achieve *natural hoof balance*; these are general trimming instructions only, however, and it is assumed the reader is already a competent trimmer and is interested in confirming hooves in their care are naturally balanced. Figures 7-1 thru 7-4 (*facing page*) summarizes the general trimming guidelines. Detailed trimming instructions are keyed to my book, *The Natural Trim: Basic Guidelines* (2019).

H°TL

H°TL is the shortest possible length of the toe wall that can be trimmed without penetrating the *hard sole plane* (HSP). H°TL defines the hoof's forward most parameter for establishing *natural hoof balance*. Until H°TL is confirmed by measuring, it is not possible, except from luck, to balance the hoof in accordance with ISNHCP natural trim guidelines. [*BG*, All of Chapter 5; Chapter 9, Step 1, p. 111.]

Hard sole plane (HSP)

Once H°TL is confirmed, the trimmer proceeds to lower the entire hoof wall to the HSP from toe to heel. Trimming, however, is preceded by the technique of "nipper dragging," a method of finding and confirming the HSP. Once this is done, attention is turned to trimming the frog and heels. [*BG*, Chapter 9, Step 2, pp. 112-113.]

Heels

Marking and balancing the heels, then trimming them to integrate with the previous trim run from toe to heel down to the HSP, concludes the process of balancing the hoof. The Balancer tool is used to mark the MLHA. Cut-lines and trimming steps are outlined in Figures 7-1 thru 7-4. [*BG*, Chapter 9, Step 3, pp. 114-115; Step 4, pp. 116-117.]

Frog

The frog also plays a key role in establishing *natural heel balance* because other nearby structures (bars, seats-of-corn, and heel buttresses) are trimmed relative to its natural size and proportions. The task here is two-fold: First, trimming the frog down to its own *hard frog plane* (HFP) — similar to the sole's *hard sole plane* (HSP). Second, if necessary, notching the frog (*Figures 3-5 and 3-6*). These actions help to determine actual heel length, which aids in finding the HFP. [*BG*, Chapter 9, Step 9, pp. 140-141.]

Natural Trim Recommendations

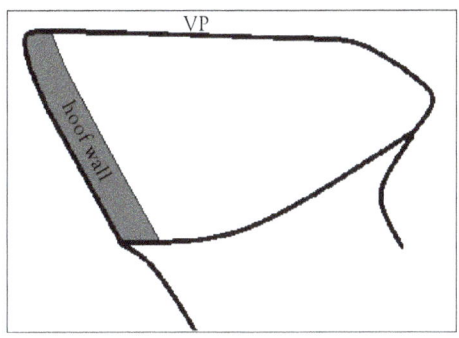

Figure 7-1. This is a simulation of an overgrown hoof. The *volar plane* (VP) is flat from toe to heel suggesting that it was shod.

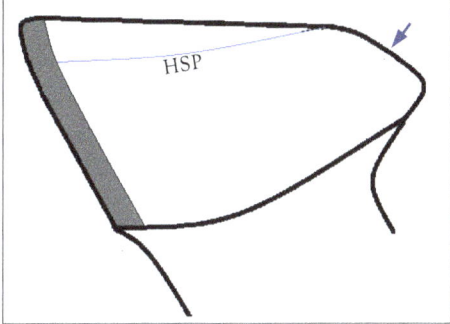

Figure 7-2. Nipper dragging has exposed the *hard sole plane* (HSP). A cut-line has been drawn from this juncture to the terminal ends of the overgrown heels. *Blue arrow* points to projected approximate location of the MLHA.

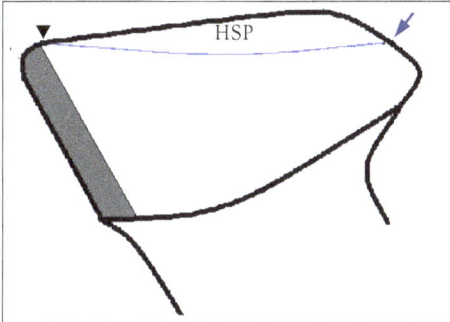

Figure 7-3. The toe wall has been shortened to the HSP. ▼ marks the location of the *medial toe wall pillar*. *Blue arrow* points to the MLHA, established by nipper dragging the HSP from the toe to the heels and frog (notched if needed). The trimmer follows the HSP (*blue line*) with the inner nipper; the outer blade will automatically adjust to the cutting path of the inner blade so as not to cut through the hoof wall and into the sole below the HSP.

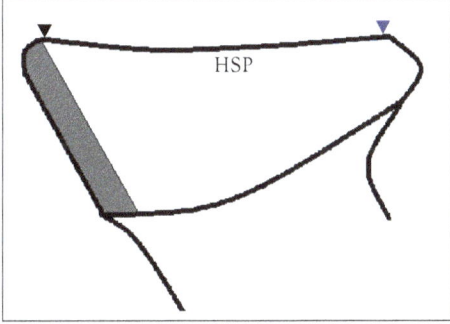

Figure 7-4. The hoof wall has been shortened to the HSP from the toe wall pillar (▼) to the heel pillar (▼). Note that the expanse of hoof wall between these pillars is slightly arched. This follows from the inner nipper blade tracing along the HSP. This arch represents passive wear, which is in keeping with the wild horse model for the naturally shaped hoof. The final step is to complete the mustang roll. [*BG*, Chapter 9, Step 5, pp. 118-131; Step 7, pp. 134-137.]

Chapter 8
Sighting Issues Due to Parallax

Positioning of the Hoof Balancer tool against the back of the hoof is critical if the MLHA is to be sighted and marked correctly. For example, if using the lower edge of the window, then the user's eye must be focused directly in line with this lower edge. The same is true if using the upper edge of the window. Allowing one's focus to drift above or below these window edges will result in a parallax shift of the MLHA, particularly if the Balancer tool were to rotate to the left or to the right, resulting in a misalignment relative to the MPVP. Remedy is through prevention: holding the Balancer tool steady against the back of the hoof while aligning its grooved line to the MPVP, and then aligning one's focus on either the upper or lower window edge will minimize or preclude any parallax shift and corruption of the MLHA. This will take practice, but also trains the eye to see independently of the Balancer tool, an important objective.

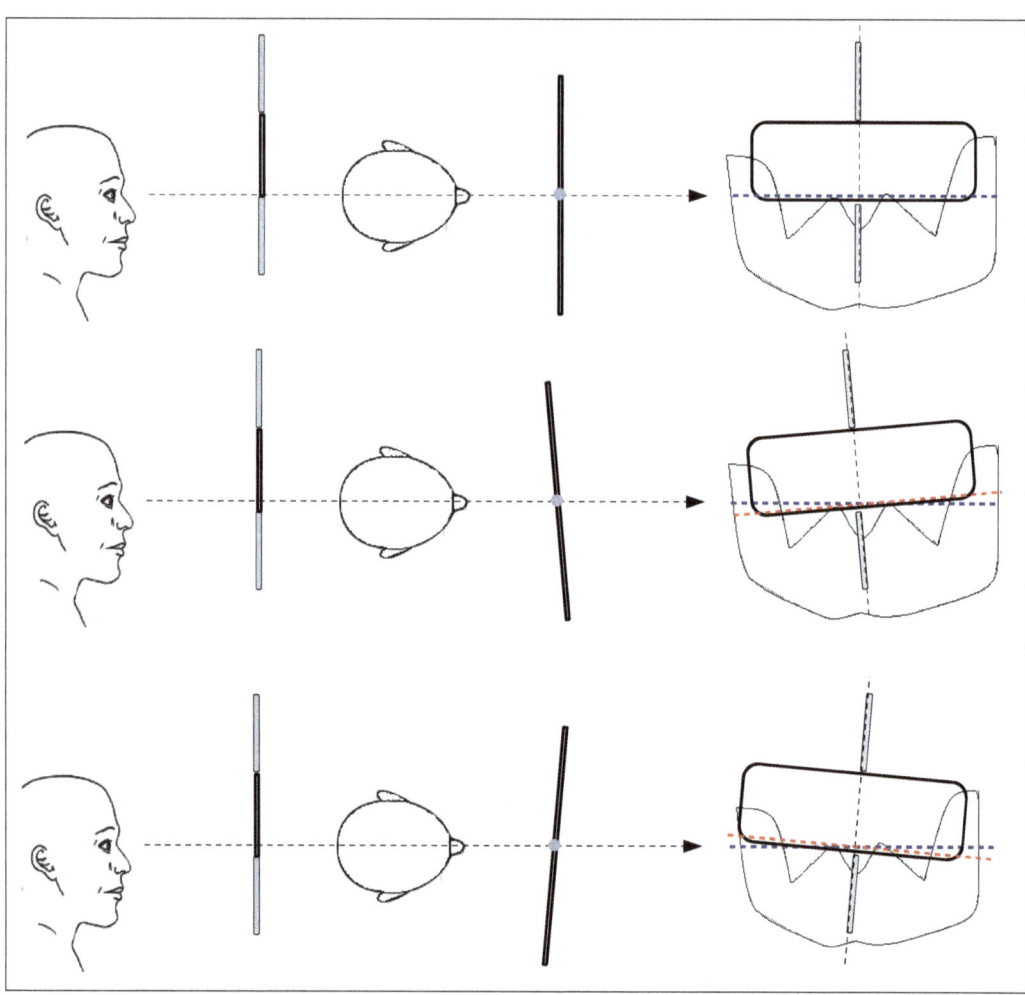

[**Figure 8-1**] Observer's focus is steady on the lower window edge of the Balancer tool, and there is no misalignment of the MLHA (*blue dashed line*).

[**Figure 8-2**]. Observer's focus has drifted inadvertently above the window edge due to a rotation of the Balancer tool towards his left eye, resulting in a parallax shift and a counterclockwise corruption of the MLHA (*red dashed line*)

[**Figure 8-3**]. A clockwise corruption of the MLHA has occurred due to a rotation of the Balancer tool toward his right eye.

Chapter 9
Care of the *Hoof Balancer Tool*

The *Hoof Balancer Tool* is made from durable polycarbonate (trade name "Lexan"). It is more scratch and break resistant than the acrylic plastics, but it is recommended that you keep it in its own protective carrier. Don't leave it around for the horse or others to step on! To clean, the tool can be washed with warm water. It can be also be cleaned and polished with polycarbonate plastic cleaners.[1]

[1] I recommend "Allstar ALL78200 Plexus Plastic Cleaner and Protectant."

Natural Horse Care Books by Jaime Jackson

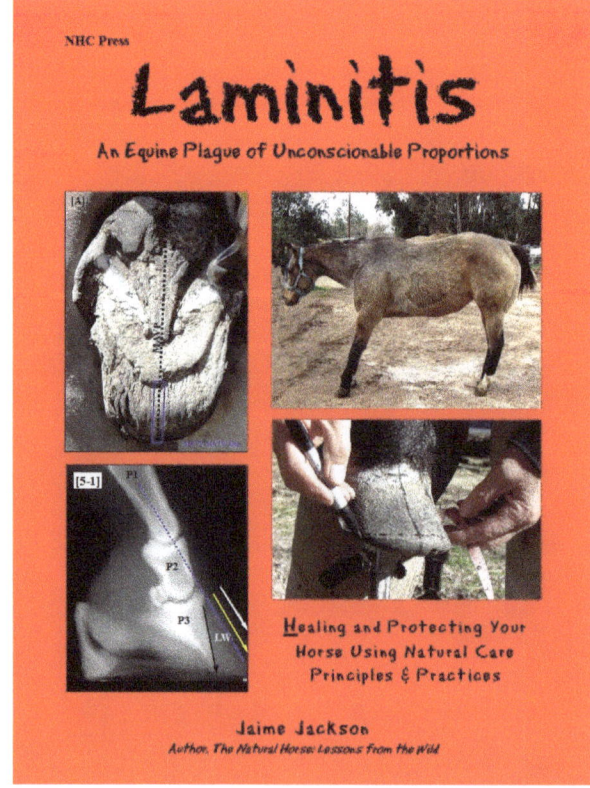

Natural Horse Care Books by Jaime Jackson

Jaime Jackson Online Store
J. Jackson Professional Tripod Hoof Stand

This hoof stand is more than just a piece of equipment for supporting the horse's hoof. It's also a sophisticated portable "work station" for carrying trimming/cleaning tools with you as you go from one hoof to the next. This hoof stand is an investment in your work and will last you for many years if taken care of and used as intended.

There are two parts to this essential equipment: The *hoof stand* that supports the hoof and weight of the horse, and its companion *tool caddy*. The hoof stand is made of plated steel to minimize rust; the caddy is made of heavy duty aluminum. The caddy rotates smoothly and quietly around the base of the hoof stand's shaft (see photo below), bringing any of the trimmer's tools within easy reach. My hoof stand and the tools/equipment on the following pages are designed to meet the specific needs of both amateur and professional (barefoot) natural hoof care providers.

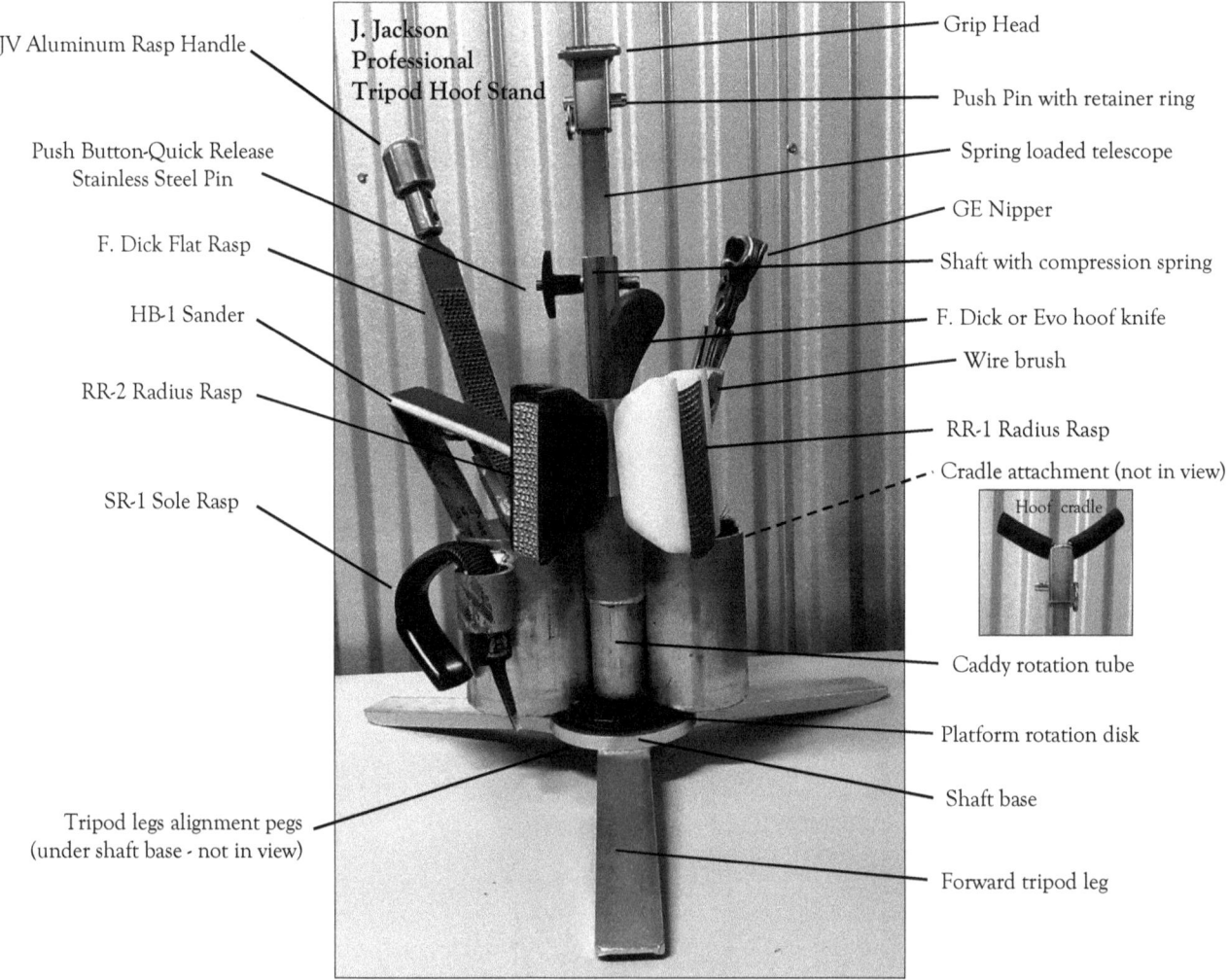

Polyethylene liner sheath for Caddy rotation tube.

Radius Rasp magnet attachment plate

Hoof knife tube

Caddy rotation tube

Rotation disk on hoof stand's shaft base.

Tool Caddy aluminum frame

Jaime Jackson Online Store
Professional Natural Trim Tools & Equipment
www.jaimejackson.com

Every barefoot trimmer needs the very best professional tools and equipment to do the best job for the horse. The natural trim is a humane trim method that mimics the natural hoof wear patterns of the wild, free-roaming horse of the U.S. Great Basin. By doing this, the trimmer unleashes natural growth patterns as seen in the wild horse hoof. The result are naturally shaped hooves that nature intended for all equines. My online store is a supply house for all the tools and equipment you will need to get these results. Home these trimming tools in the caddy of your J. Jackson Professional Tripod Hoof Stand.

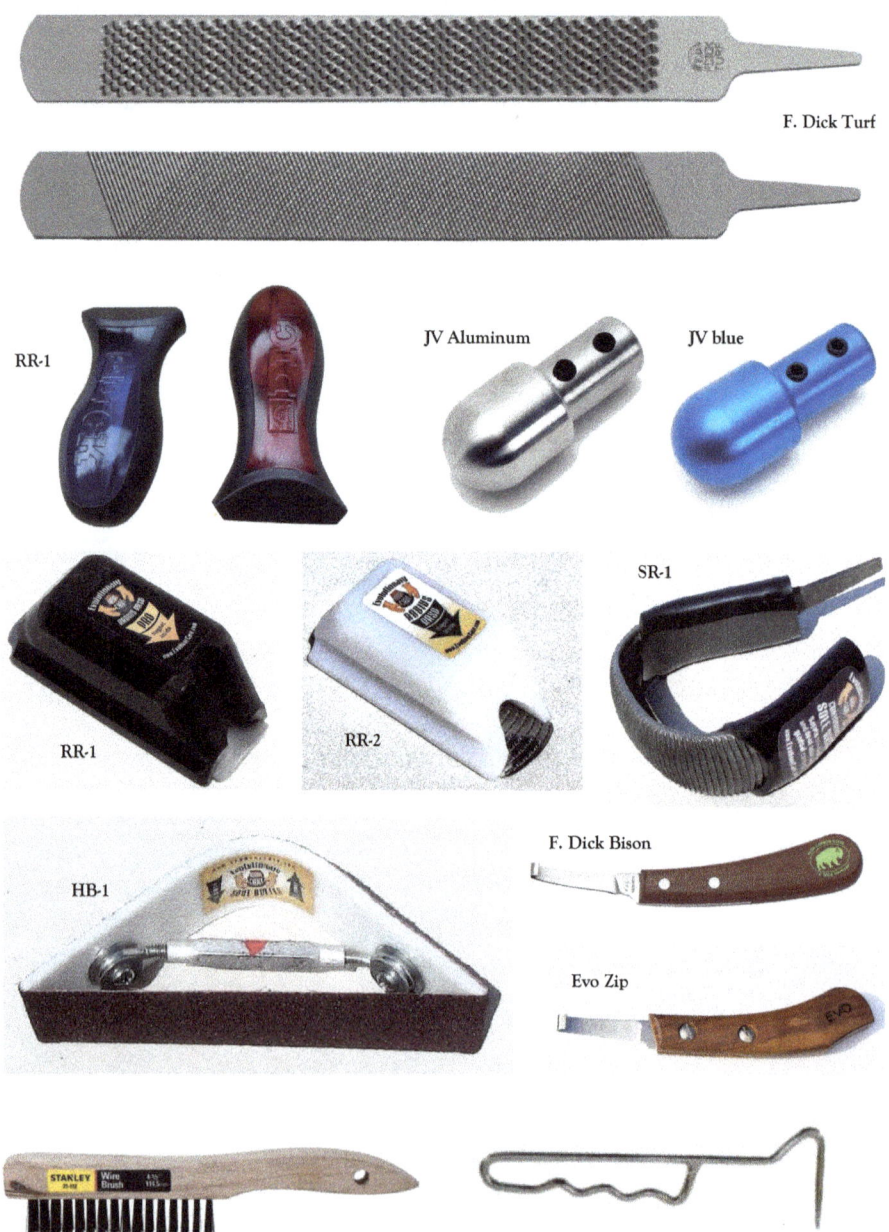

F. Dick "Turf" Flat Rasp — I am a long time advocate and seller of the F. Dick Company's flat rasp. F. Dick is a prominent, centuries old German cutlery manufacturer with a sideline in hoof care tools. This rasp is aggressive, sharp, and well-balanced, unrivaled among flat rasps in my opinion.

Rasp handles — I carry two high quality brands: the new ultra-modern F. Dick hammer-on in red-black and blue-black; and the JV-Aluminum in red, blue, and aluminum colors, which are set with a supplied Allen wrench.

Radius Rasps and Sole Rasp — The Evo RR-1 and RR-2 are key players in forming the eponymous Mustang Roll. The SR-1 is deployed to remove excess solar plates and overgrown bars.

Bow Sander and Hoof Knives — The Evo HB-1 bow sander/buffer is used to fine finish the Mustang Roll and buff the outer wall. The ergonometric F. Dick Bison and Evo Zip knives possess razor sharp steel blades and hardwood handles.

Hoof cleaning tools — I recommend my wire brush and professional hoof pick with grip handle for efficient hoof cleaning.

Hoof Nippers — I offer the GE Forge 14-inch "Easy" Nipper, drop-forged from chrome vanadium steel; and the 12-inch Evo Spring Powered Nipper. Either facilitates ultra-precision when cutting the mustang roll and general ease of trimming.

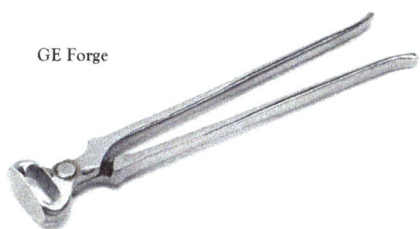
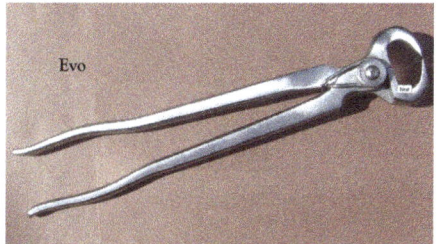

Hoof gauges — The (*left to right*) 6-inch Vernier Caliper, Hoof Balancer, and Hoof Meter Reader are natural trim essentials for determining capsule size, proportion, and balance.

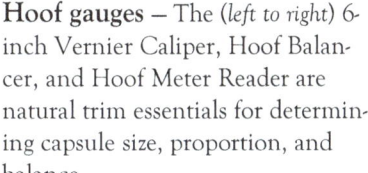
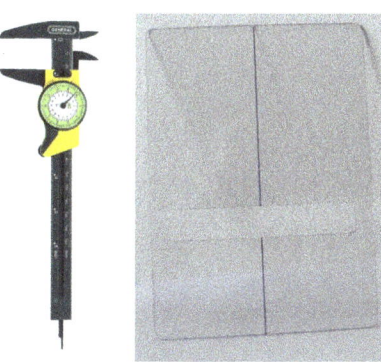
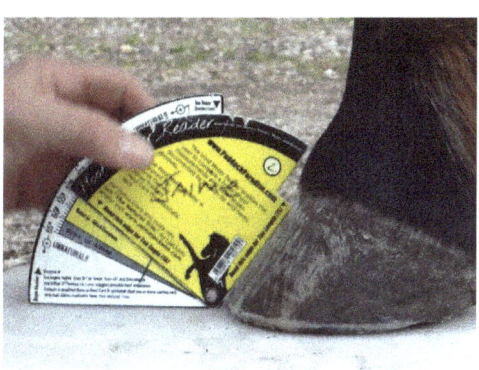

Trimmer's Apron — I have these made to order from the highest quality leather, stainless steel hardware, and artisan workmanship. Fits men and women equally well, with adjustable belt and leg straps. Reinforced thighs with duel left/right holsters for my professional hoof pick or hoof knives.

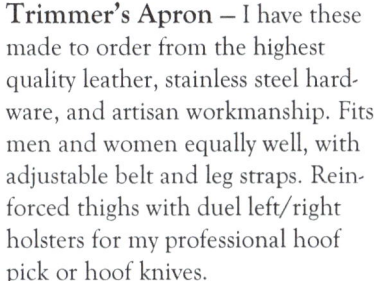

Rope Halters — Halters are essential "tools" for what is called "Sequencing" during the natural trim. Used skillfully, these halters facilitate communication between the trimmer and the horse, enabling the trimmer to command the horse's attention and body positions during trimming and when transitioning from one hoof to the next.

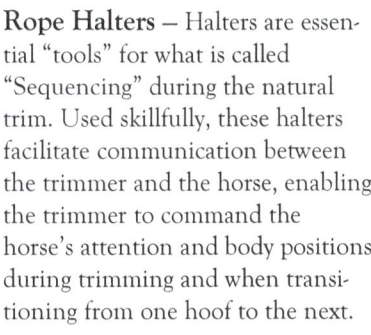

Jaime Jackson Online Store
Hay Poles and Hay Bags for Paddock Paradise
www.jaimejackson.com

Essential to natural hoof care is natural horse care in the broadest sense, including natural boarding, known as "Paddock Paradise" among NHC advocates. My book of the same name is an important flagship in the natural care revolution. I have designed a new product for feeding horses in the Paddock Paradise habitat: hay poles from which hay bags are hung. This manner of feeding horses enables the horse owner to control the types and quantities of hay forage to be fed. Horses can eat at anytime in the Paddock Paradise tracking system. Hay waste is also minimized. I offer two hay pole systems:

Netted hay bag

Hay Pole for Netted Hay Bags

This hay pole system uses netted hay bags. My hay poles come fully assembled. The hay poles are set over standard t-posts, which you supply. Pack and clip the netted hay bags at your barn and then take them to your track and snap them onto your hay poles in seconds. Your horses will take it from there! See downloadable instructions on my website.

  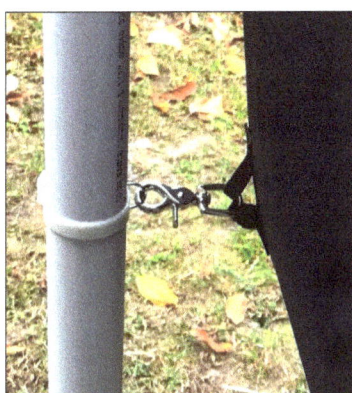 

Gusseted hay bag. Horses can forage from top and/or from center hole on front side of bag.

Easy hay packing!

Hay Pole for Gusseted Hay Bags (with foraging hole)

This hay pole uses a gusseted hay bag. Hay poles come fully assembled.

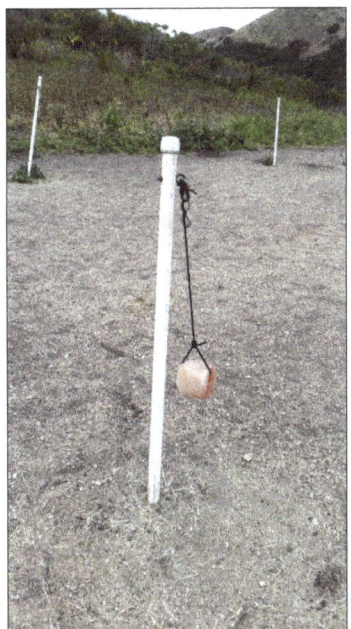  

Hang your salt lick from a hay pole!

T-Post Disk

Downward pressure applied to the hay bag by the horse when eating can drive the hay pole and t-post into the ground, especially soft or wet ground, which can soil and ruin the hay. My metal *t-post disks* can help solve this problem. The horse's pressure will now transfer from the hay pole to the disk, which will prevent the hay pole and t-post from sinking any further into the ground.

NHC Social Media

www.AANHCP.net
Association for the Advancement of Natural Horse Care Practices
NHC Advocacy, Articles, Support, Links

This is the official website of the AANHCP. Here you will find a history of the organization, its legal status and vital mission, officers, NHC practitioners, and articles of interest. Founded in 2000, our members have pioneered the international natural horse care revolution ever since.

www.ISNHCP.net
Institute for the Study of Natural Horse Care Practices

The ISNHCP provides professional level training for natural hoof care practitioners based on Jaime Jackson's research of America's wild, free-roaming horses, and countless applications with proven results on domesticated horses over nearly 40 years.

NHC Facebook Pages
AANHCP · ISNHCP · Paddock Paradise
J. Jackson NHC Services · The Natural Trim

Image Credits

Christopher Pollitt, *7*

Jill Willis, *13, 14, 17*

Rhonda Mullins, *31*

All other images by the author.

www.ingramcontent.com/pod-product-compliance
Lightning Source LLC
Chambersburg PA
CBHW040731020526
44112CB00058B/2931